Basic Communication Strategies II

Julyan Nutt   Adam Huston   Manabu Miyata   Yoko Kurahashi

SANSHUSHA

Preface

Basic Communication Strategies is a comprehensive two-book English conversation textbook tailored specifically for Japanese non-English major university students. As the name suggests, the series focuses on learning the basic communication strategies needed to hold meaningful conversations in English.

Each textbook comprises six units—divided into Part A and Part B, centered around everyday conversation topics, and taught over two weeks—and two review units. The title of each unit is one of the opening questions introduced at the beginning of Part A. The same question will be revisited as a conversation starter to the second speaking activity at the end of the corresponding Part B. The authors' aim is that, after learning essential vocabulary, inputting that vocabulary in model conversations, practicing through speaking, listening and pronunciation activities, and learning communication strategies, students will be better able to hold a simple conversation on the unit topic than they were at the beginning of the unit. The authors propose to evaluate this by conducting individual bi-semester speaking tests while the class completes the review units. To provide the teacher with another opportunity for evaluation, and the student with progress feedback, each Part B starts with a five-minute quiz to review the material covered in the previous Part A.

Additionally, some instructions are provided in Japanese, and there is a comprehensive Japanese glossary at the end of the textbooks, with the aim of maximizing classroom efficiency.

音声ダウンロード＆ストリーミングサービス(無料)のご案内

https://www.sanshusha.co.jp/text/onsei/isbn/9784384335361/

本書の音声データは、上記アドレスよりダウンロードおよびストリーミング再生ができます。ぜひご利用ください。

本書の構成と特徴

　本書は『ベーシック・コミュニケーション』のブック 2 に当たります。Preface にあるように、主として英語を専門としない学生を対象としており、英語での会話をスムーズに進めるためのテキストです。著者であるネイティブ・スピーカー 2 人が日本で大学生を教えてきた長年の経験に基づき、大学生にとって必要とされるのはどのような英語か、また、どのようにすれば会話を楽しめるかということを念頭において編集されています。本書の構成を特徴とともに紹介すると、以下のようになります。

① 全 6 ユニットから成り、それぞれのユニットタイトルがそのユニットで取り組むトピックを示しています。

② 各ユニットは [Part A] と [Part B] に分かれ、[Part A] でモデルとなる会話や表現を学び、[Part B] でそれを実際に用いる言語活動を行って、自由に会話を楽しんで終わる、という構成になっています。

③ [Part A] では、役に立つ表現の学習、モデルの対話文を用いた会話練習、関連する文法事項の学習、ペアまたはグループで行うスピーチ活動、と順に取り組んで、必要な英語力・会話力を身につけます。

④ [Part B] では、基本表現の確認問題、発音やイントネーションの練習、リスニング問題に取り組んだあとで、会話を進めるための方略を学び、ユニットタイトルのトピックについて、自由に会話をして締めくくります。

⑤ 3 つのユニットを終えると、復習のための Review Unit があります。それまでの学習の成果を測るために、担当の教員が個人面接をする際に用いるトピックが最初に設けてありますので、準備をしてください。これに続く、クロスワードパズルの問題、発話に応答する問題、読解問題は、クラスメートが面接を受けている間に各自で取り組みます。

⑥ 最初の Review Unit 1 が終わると、同じように 3 つのユニットと Review Unit 2 で学習します。こうして、各ユニットに 2 回の授業（計 12 回）、Review Unit に 2 回の授業、合計 14 回の授業で本書を用いた学習ができるようになっています。

⑦ 本書では、活動の指示文や文法に関する重要なポイントについて、日本語の説明が加えてあります。必要に応じて参照してください。

⑧ 巻末に、2 種類の語彙リストが掲載されています。1 つは "Useful Expressions" で、各ユニット [Part A] のセクション 2 に出てくる重要表現を整理して、英和索引（アルファベット順）および和英索引（アイウエオ順）にしてあります。もう 1 つは "Words & Phrases" で、テキストに出てくる語句のうち必要と思われるものを選び出し、アルファベット順にまとめました。各ユニットの英文や解説がわからないときに利用してください。

　本書を用いた学習を通じて、英語による会話のキャッチボールがスムーズにできるようになることを願っています。

著者一同

Table of Contents

Preface

Unit 1 Are you still in touch with your friends from junior high?

Part A   6

- Useful Expressions
- Present perfect
- Model Conversation
- Speaking 1: **Find someone who...**

Part B   10

- Quiz
- Rejoinders
- Contractions of the auxiliary *have*
- Speaking 2: **Old school friends**

Unit 2 What do you do to stay healthy?

Part A   16

- Useful Expressions
- Countable/uncountable noun qualifiers
- Model Conversation
- Speaking 1: **Health survey**

Part B   20

- Quiz
- Rejoinders and follow-up questions
- The schwa sound in questions
- Speaking 2: **About health**

Unit 3 What is your ideal job for the future?

Part A   26

- Useful Expressions
- Prepositions, Adjectives
- Model Conversation
- Speaking 1: **Resume questionnaire**

Part B   31

- Quiz
- Asking for explanation or clarification
- Stressed syllables
- Speaking 2: **Interview for a job**

Review 1 Interview Test / Exercises   36

Unit 4 What was the greatest day of your life?

Part A   40

- Useful Expressions
- Relative clauses
- Model Conversation
- Speaking 1: **Missing information**

Part B   44

- Quiz
- Asking for detail
- Intonation and rhythm
- Speaking 2: **Greatest day of your life**

Unit 5 Where is somewhere you would like to visit?

Part A   48

- Useful Expressions
- Verb of perception
- Model Conversation
- Speaking 1: **Board game**

Part B   53

- Quiz
- Suggestions with support
- Assimilation of *you* with auxiliary verbs
- Speaking 2: **Planning a trip**

Unit 6 What is something you feel strongly about?

Part A   58

- Useful Expressions
- Adverbs for emphasis
- Model Conversation
- Speaking 1: **Exchange of opinions**

Part B   62

- Quiz
- Getting people to respond
- Function words at the end
- Speaking 2: **Discussion**

Review 2 Interview Test / Exercises   67

Worksheet for Student B (Unit 4)   71

Glossary Useful Expressions   74

        Words & Phrases   76

Unit 1 — Are you still in touch with your friends from junior high?

Part A

Section 1 — Opening Questions

▶ Ask your partner the following questions. Remember to answer yes/no questions with extra information.
会話の相手に次の質問をしなさい。「はい／いいえ」で答える場合には、情報を追加して答えるようにしましょう。

1. Are you still in touch with your friends from junior high?
2. Who is your best friend? When was the last time you met him/her?
3. How have you been spending your free time recently?
4. Who have you been hanging out with?

Section 2 — Useful Expressions

▶ Connect the expressions in **bold** to match them to the Japanese meaning.

1. I did not **keep** ［〜と連絡を取り合う］
2. Please **drop** ［〜に連絡する］
3. What **have** you **been** ［〜していた］
4. I **lost** ［連絡が取れなくなった］
5. I **bumped** ［〜と偶然出会った］

a. **up to** lately?
b. **contact** with my high school friends.
c. **in touch with** my younger brother.
d. me **a line** after class.
e. **into** my teacher in the park.

1. _____   2. _____   3. _____   4. _____   5. _____

6

Section 3 Model Conversation

Exercise 1

 001

▶ Two old friends are meeting after a long time. Listen to and read their conversation.

Linda: Hey Steve, long time, no see.
Steve: Hello, Linda. How have you been?
Linda: (1)Good, thanks. And you?
Steve: (2)Fine, thank you.
Linda: So, what have you been up to?
Steve: Mostly (3)going to school and playing baseball. What about you?
Linda: Just (4)studying and working part time.
Steve: Well, drop me a line some time.
Linda: Yes, let's (5)keep in touch.
Steve: (6)Definitely.
Linda: I'll give you a call (7)sometime next week.
Steve: That would be great.

Exercise 2

▶ Practice the conversation with your partner. First, substitute the underlined parts in the model conversation as below. Next, try to substitute them with your own ideas.

Substitution	Your idea
1. Very well, thank you	1. _____
2. Great, thanks	2. _____
3. hanging out with friends	3. _____
4. working and going to the gym in the evening	4. _____
5. stay in contact	5. _____
6. Of course	6. _____
7. in the next couple of weeks	7. _____

Section 4 | Language Focus

Exercise 1

▶ Your best friend calls you and asks how you are. Based on the situation, choose a correct response from the box. There may be more than one answer.

> Amazing ✦ Pretty good ✦ Really good, actually
> Not so good ✦ ~~Not bad~~ ✦ Terrible, to be honest

1. You feel fine, the same as usual. *Not bad* _____.

2. You have a fever and a headache. _____.

3. Your dog has just died. _____.

4. You just heard you got a good grade for your report. _____.

5. You are excited about starting your summer vacation. _____.

6. It's Monday morning. _____.

7. You are going to a live music concert. _____.

Exercise 2

▶ Change the present tense into the present perfect.

1. How are you?

   How have you been? _____

2. Are you well?

   _____

3. How's it going?

   _____

4. What are you up to?

   _____

5. Where are you living?

   _____

6. How's work?

   _____

7. How's your family?

   _____

8. Are you studying hard?

   _____

Unit 1

9. Are you living in Osaka?

_____

Section 5 Speaking 1—Find someone who ...

▶ Find out what your classmates have been doing recently.

Exercise 1

▶ First, make yes/no questions, and then think of suitable follow-up questions.

Exercise 2

▶ Ask your classmates. Find a different person for each question.

Find someone who ...		
Convert the following into yes/no questions	Name	Follow-up question
1. ... has had a nice vacation <u>Have you had a nice vacation</u> ?	Kenji	What did you do?
2. ... has been abroad _____ ?		
3. ... has been studying hard _____ ?		
4. ... has done anything fun _____ ?		
5. ... has been working part time a lot _____ ?		
6. ... has met any friends _____ ?		
7. ... has tried anything new _____ ?		
8. ... has been busy _____ ?		
9. ... has been spending time with their family _____ ?		
10. ... has met someone interesting _____ ?		

9

Part B

Section 1 Quiz

▶ Choose the correct words to complete the sentences.

> be ✦ been ✦ bump ✦ drop ✦ gone
> hang ✦ keep ✦ lose ✦ mostly ✦ spend

1. John will be a little late. He has _____ to the bathroom.
2. Have you ever _____ to a foreign country?
3. Recently, I've been _____ing out with friends after class.
4. I really enjoy _____ing time with my family on weekends.
5. I feel terrible, to _____ honest.
6. Please _____ me a line if you have time.
7. It is important to _____ in touch with your old friends.
8. It is important not to _____ contact with your old friends.
9. Guess who I _____ed into yesterday!
10. I _____ work on weekday evenings.

Score: _____ / 10

Section 2 Pronunciation—Contractions of the auxiliary *have*

 002

When we speak using the perfect form, the auxiliary verb *have/has/had* is often contracted (See examples 1 and 2). When *have* is used as the main verb, it is not contracted (See example 3).

完了形の助動詞 have/has/had は、よく短縮されます（例 1・2 参照）。have を動詞として使う場合は、**短縮できません**（例 3 参照）。

e.g.
1. She has broken a bone. → She's broken a bone. ✓
2. I had been studying. → I'd been studying. ✓
3. Tom has a cat. → Tom's a cat. ✗

Unit 1

The auxiliary *have* is also contracted in the question form.
助動詞 have は疑問詞の後にくるときにも短縮されることがあります。

what have → what've	what has → what's
where have → where've	where has → where's
when have → when've	when has → when's
who have → who've	who has → who's
how have → how've	how has → how's

e.g. 4. Where have you been? → Where've you been?
5. Who has eaten my cookie? → Who's eaten my cookie?

Exercise 1

 003

▶ Listen to the following questions or statements. Some are contracted, some are not. Fill in the blanks with either *have*, *'ve*, *has*, *'s*, *had*, or *'d*.

1. What _____ you been up to?
2. He _____ been studying.
3. How _____ you been?
4. Tony _____ broken his leg.
5. There _____ been an accident on the highway.
6. How long _____ you known him?
7. _____ you seen the new Spiderman movie?
8. I _____ not been feeling well recently.
9. They _____ a busy weekend.
10. Do you _____ a test next week?

Exercise 2

▶ Practice reading the questions and statements with your partner.

Exercise 3

▶ Practice reading the Model Conversation of **Section 3** of **Part A** (p. 7). This time try to use the contracted form of *have*.

11

Section 3 Listening

🎧 004, 005

▶ Listen to two people who have met someone after a long time. Complete the information.

	Listening 1	Listening 2
Who did the person meet?		
What information do we hear about that person? Write as much information as you can.		

Unit 1

Section 4 Communication Strategy—Rejoinders

We use rejoinders to encourage the speaker to continue.

Exercise 1

🎧 004, 005

▶ Listen to **Section 3**: **Listening** again. What rejoinders do you hear? Circle them.

I see. ✦ Mm-hmm. ✦ No way! ✦ Oh. ✦ Oh, dear. ✦ Oh, yeah? ✦ That's great!
That's too bad. ✦ Really? ✦ Right. ✦ Sure. ✦ Uh-huh. ✦ Yeah?

Exercise 2

▶ Complete the following conversations with rejoinders from above. There may be more than one answer.

Conversation 1

A: I have some good news.

B: _____

A: I passed my English test.

B: _____ I thought you said it was difficult.

A: It was, but I could pass it!

B: _____ Well done!

A: Thanks.

Conversation 2

A: It's going to rain tomorrow.

B: _____

A: So, we'll have to cancel our picnic.

B: _____ I was looking forward to that.

A: Me, too. Let's go next weekend.

B: _____ That's a good idea.

A: Great.

💬 Practice these conversations with your partner.

13

Exercise 3

▶ Have free conversations on these topics:

| My best friend | My pet | My hobby | My family |

Student A	Student B
• Choose one topic from above. • Try to talk about the topic for one or two minutes. • Leave a small break after each sentence.	• Listen carefully to your partner. • Add an appropriate rejoinder after each sentence to encourage your partner to keep talking.

💬 Reverse roles and have two more conversations.

Section 5 — Speaking 2

▶ Conversation Goal—Have a conversation with your partner about your old school friends. Ask at least four follow-up questions each.

以前の学校の友人について会話しなさい。各自、追加の質問を少なくとも4つしましょう。

Conversation Starter: Are you still in touch with your friends from junior high?

- **Show interest when your partner is talking by using rejoinders:** No way. Really? That's too bad. Mm-hmm.
- **Ask follow-up questions about each other's school friends.**
- **Be careful with contractions.**

Take notes about your partner(s) and present your results/findings to a group and/or the class.

Unit 2 What do you do to stay healthy?

Part A

Section 1 Opening Questions

▶ Ask your partner the following questions. Remember to answer yes/no questions with extra information.

1. What do you do to stay healthy? How often do you do that?
2. Have you ever been on a diet? Was it successful?
3. Is there anything you should change about your lifestyle?
4. Is there any food you can't eat?

Section 2 Useful Expressions

▶ Connect the expressions in **bold** to match them to the Japanese meaning.

1. Tom **looks good** ［年の割には元気そう］
2. Andrew feels he is **out of** ［体調が悪い］
3. I'd like to **experiment** ［〜を試してみる］
4. David sometimes **skips** ［食事を抜く］
5. I am not **in** ［健康で］

a. **shape** recently.
b. **with** my hair a little.
c. **a meal** when he is busy.
d. **for** his **age**.
e. **good health.**

1. _____   2. _____   3. _____   4. _____   5. _____

| | Unit 2 |

Section 3 (Model Conversation

Exercise 1

🎧 006

▶ Two friends are talking about their lifestyles. Listen to and read their conversation.

Kosuke: What do you do to stay in shape?

Robert: I've been experimenting with a new (1)lifestyle.

Kosuke: Oh, yeah? How does it work?

Robert: Well, I (2)skip breakfast in the morning and (3)go for a long walk three times a week.

Kosuke: That's great. So, have you lost any weight?

Robert: (4)Only a kilogram.

Kosuke: I'm (5)out of shape, so I guess I should join you.

Robert: Maybe you should start by (6)cutting out junk food.

Kosuke: Yeah, that's a good place to start.

Robert: And let me know if you want to (7)try some of my new healthy recipes.

Kosuke: Okay, I will.

Exercise 2

▶ Practice the conversation with your partner. First, substitute the underlined parts in the model conversation as below. Next, try to substitute them with your own ideas.

Substitution	Your idea
1. exercise routine	1. _____
2. go for a run before work	2. _____
3. go to the gym after work	3. _____
4. Almost five kilograms	4. _____
5. not very fit	5. _____
6. exercising a little more	6. _____
7. join my gym	7. _____

17

| Section 4 | Language Focus |

Exercise 1

▶ Choose the correct word to complete the sentences.

1. I have been attempting (to / ~~with~~) lose weight.

2. The government is experimenting (with / by) a four-day working week.

3. You should be careful (about / at) how you spend your money.

4. If you cut (down / out) on the amount of salt you eat, it is better for your health.

5. Sara has been feeling better since she cut (down / out) junk food from her diet.

6. Being (in / on) a diet can be tough when you go out to eat.

7. I could not deal (with / for) the stress very well.

Exercise 2

▶ Complete the sentences using countable/uncountable noun qualifiers from the box.
下の枠内の加算名詞／不可算名詞につく修飾語（＝形容詞）を使用して文を完成しなさい。

Countable	Uncountable
(a) few	(a) little
~~fewer~~	less
many	much
several (some)	some

1. This year the number of students in my class is small. There are ___*fewer*___ students than last year.

2. The students complained about the amount of homework. It was too _____ for them.

3. Takeshi tried to contact his teacher _____ times, but the teacher did not reply to his message.

4. The training room did not have _____ equipment to exercise with.

5. The textbook was quite cheap. It cost a lot _____ than Anna thought.

6. I have _____ assignments to complete by next week—at least three.

7. I like to do _____ stretching every night before I go to bed.

8. Hurry up! We only have _____ time. There's only _____ minutes before the show starts.

Unit **2**

Section 5 Speaking 1—Health survey

▶ Complete the following survey and then interview one classmate to find how healthy you both are.

Health survey
1. How often do you exercise? **a.** Less than once a week. **b.** About once a week. **c.** More than three times a week. **2.** How many hours do you usually sleep at night? **a.** Fewer than 6 hours or more than 9 hours.   **b.** 6 to 7 hours.   **c.** 7 to 9 hours. **3.** What time do you go to sleep? **a.** After midnight. **b.** Between 11 p.m. and midnight. **c.** Usually before 11 p.m. **4.** How often do you eat junk food? **a.** 2 or 3 times a day.   **b.** 2 or 3 times a week.   **c.** Less than once a week. **5.** Do you eat vegetables with your meals? **a.** No, I hardly ever do.   **b.** Only with some of my meals.   **c.** Yes, I usually do. **6.** How many cups of coffee do you drink a day? **a.** 3 or more cups a day.   **b.** About 1 cup a day.   **c.** I usually drink water or tea. **7.** Do you smoke or drink alcohol? **a.** Yes, I often smoke or drink alcohol. **b.** Yes, I sometimes smoke or drink alcohol. **c.** No, I don't do either. **8.** Do you feel stressed? **a.** Yes, a lot.   **b.** Yes, sometimes.   **c.** Yes, but only a little.

▶ Look at the scoring system below. And count your total number of points. Compare your points in groups of four. Who is the healthiest? What can you do to improve your health?

	RED	**YELLOW**	**GREEN**
Scoring system:	a. = -2 points	b. = 1 point	c. = 2 points

RED —You should seriously try to change this habit.

YELLOW —You are doing okay, but you could try harder to improve this habit.

GREEN —You are doing well, but try hard to continue this great habit.

Part B

Section 1 Quiz

▶ Circle the correct words to complete the sentences.

1. The doctor said I must cut (down / out) junk food completely.
2. I need to cut (down / out) on the (amount / number) of salt I eat.
3. The (amount / number) of foreign people visiting Japan is increasing.
4. I will be (in / on) a diet before my wedding.
5. Exercising three times a week helps me be (in / on) good shape.
6. I have been experimenting (at / with) a non-fat diet.
7. The teacher has to deal (at / with) (many / much) problems.
8. I don't have (many / much) time to go to the gym.

Score: _____ / 10

Section 2 Pronunciation—The schwa sound in questions

▶ Listen to this question carefully.

What do you do to stay in shape?

Which words are stressed? These are the content words of the sentence. They convey their meanings. (Content words: nouns, adjectives, verbs, adverbs, etc.)

上の文で強勢が置かれている単語は内容語で、実質的な意味を含んでいます。(内容語：名詞、形容詞、動詞、副詞など)

What do you do to stay in shape?

Now listen to the vowel sounds in the remaining words of the sentence. They are function words and are not voiced. This sound is known as the schwa vowel. (Function words: pronouns, articles, prepositions, conjunctions, etc.)

内容語以外の単語は機能語で、母音が無声化されます。それを「あいまい母音」と呼んでいます。(機能語：代名詞、冠詞、前置詞、接続詞など)

What d' y' do t' stay 'n shape?

Unit 2

Exercise 1

 008

▶ Listen to the following questions/statements. Can you identify the stressed words? Underline them.

1. When do you get to school?
2. My brother's not as tall as me.
3. How many cups of tea do you drink a day?
4. I'm here for the class.
5. What time do you go to sleep?
6. Is this your bike?
7. Do you eat rice with your meals?
8. Have you seen my wallet?

Exercise 2

▶ Listen to the questions/statements again. Can you identify the schwa vowels? Circle them. Practice saying the sentences with your partner.

Exercise 3

009

▶ Listen to the questions or statements. Fill in the missing words.

1. _____ brother _____ sister _____ America.
2. What _____ do _____ car?
3. _____ students _____ apartments.
4. _____ many people like _____ dogs.
5. _____ want _____ go _____ bathroom?
6. I want _____ get _____ coffee.

💬 Practice saying the sentences with your partner.

21

Section 3　Listening

Exercise 1

 010

▶ Lucy and Claire are in a restaurant. They are discussing what they are going to order. What food do they decide to order? Listen to the conversation.

Lucy		
	Order	Reason
Main		
Dessert		

Claire		
	Order	Reason
Main		
Dessert		

Exercise 2

▶ Listen again. What reasons do they give for choosing those two dishes?

Unit 2

Section 4 | Communication Strategy
—Asking follow-up questions to encourage the speaker to give more detail

Exercise 1

▶ Look at the Model Conversation from **Section 3** of **Part A** (p. 17). What rejoinder +
follow-up question combinations are used?

- _____

- _____

Exercise 2

▶ Look at the four example conversations. Choose a suitable rejoinder from below and
predict B's possible follow-up question.

> I see. ✦ Mm-hmm. ✦ No way! ✦ Oh. ✦ Oh, dear. ✦ Oh, yeah? ✦ That's great!
> That's too bad. ✦ Really? ✦ Right. ✦ Sure. ✦ Uh-huh. ✦ Yeah?

1. A: I'm from the UK.

B: _____   _____?

A: A beautiful city called York.

2. A: I've lived in Japan for a long time.

B: _____   _____?

A: For about 20 years.

3. A: I don't like rock music.

B: _____   _____?

A: It's too noisy.

4. A: I can play two musical instruments.

B: _____   _____?

A: The trumpet and the trombone.

23

Exercise 3

▶ Take turns responding to the other student's question with a rejoinder and a follow-up question. The other student does not have to answer the follow-up questions.
The first few question types have been chosen for you. Speak, don't write.

Student A		Student B
1. I'm from a big family.	➡	_____ How many _____?
2. _____ Where _____?	⬅	I like my hometown.
3. I love sports.	➡	_____ What _____?
4. _____ Why _____?	⬅	I am so tired.
5. I speak two languages.	➡	_____ _____?
6. _____ _____?	⬅	I have been to many countries.
7. I am busy on the weekend.	➡	_____ _____?
8. _____ _____?	⬅	I had an accident yesterday.

Exercise 4

▶ Have free conversations on these topics:

My school   My part-time job   My club   My dream

Student A	Student B
• Choose one topic from above. • Try to talk about the topic for one or two minutes. • Leave a small break after each sentence. • Try to answer your partner's follow-up questions.	• Listen carefully to your partner. • Add an appropriate rejoinder and follow-up question after each sentence to encourage your partner to keep talking.

💬 Reverse roles and have two more conversations.

24

Section 5 Speaking 2

▶ Conversation Goal—Have a conversation with your partner about health. Find three things you have in common.
健康について会話しなさい。2 人に共通していることを 3 つ見つけましょう。

Conversation Starter: What do you do to stay healthy?

Hints

- **Remember to stress content words:** **What** do you **do** to **stay** in **shape**?
- **Remember the unvoiced schwa sound:** What d' y' do t' stay 'n shape?
- **Try to add rejoinders and follow-up questions:** Really? How often do you go?

Take notes about your partner(s) and present your results/findings to a group and/or the class.

Unit 3 What is your ideal job for the future?

Part A

Section 1 Opening Questions

▶ Ask your partner the following questions. Remember to answer yes/no questions with extra information.

1. Have you ever had a part-time job? What kind of job?
2. Are you interested in doing an internship?
3. Do you prefer working with other people or working alone?
4. What is your ideal job for the future?

Section 2 Useful Expressions

▶ Connect the expressions in **bold** to match them to the Japanese meaning.

1. It is good to **be involved** ［〜と関わり合う］
2. I **am** not **good** ［〜するのが得意］
3. People say I **have good** ［コミュニケーション力がある］
4. I always **put in** ［〜に努力を注ぐ］
5. Yuki **is good** ［〜の扱いがうまい］

a. **communication skills**.
b. **with** small children.
c. **at** solving problems.
d. **in** your community.
e. **effort with** my work.

1. _____   2. _____   3. _____   4. _____   5. _____

26

Unit 3

| Section 3 | Model Conversation

Exercise 1

🎧 011

▶ Yuichi is applying for an internship. Listen to and read their conversation.

Interviewer: So, why would you like to work here?

Yuichi: I have always been interested in (1)retail.

Interviewer: Mm-hmm.

Yuichi: And after I graduate, I would like to work in (2)sales.

Interviewer: I see. Do you have any experience (3)dealing with customers?

Yuichi: Well, (4)I helped my parents in their restaurant when I was (5)in high school.

Interviewer: That's good.

Yuichi: And people say (6)I have good communication skills.

Interviewer: That will be useful. So …, do you have any questions?

Yuichi: Yes. (7)Will there be overtime?

Interviewer: Let's discuss that at the next meeting.

Yuichi: Okay. Thank you.

Exercise 2

▶ Practice the conversation with your partner. First, substitute the underlined parts in the model conversation as below. Next, try to substitute them with your own ideas.

Substitution	Your idea
1. teaching	**1.** _____
2. education	**2.** _____
3. teaching children	**3.** _____
4. I volunteered at my local elementary school	**4.** _____
5. in the second year	**5.** _____
6. I am good at explaining things	**6.** _____
7. Do you know when I can start?	**7.** _____

Section 4 Language Focus

Exercise 1

▶ Choose the correct preposition for the following sentences.

1. Mary is good (at / ~~with~~) math. She always gets top grades.
2. Alice is good (at / with) numbers. She never makes mistakes.
3. She was bad (at / for) drawing. Her pictures were like a child's.
4. Dealing (in / with) customers can be difficult.
5. James is involved (at / in) the local community.
6. My teacher told me I need to put in more effort (for / with) my homework.

Exercise 2

▶ Choose the correct personality trait to match its dictionary definition.

> ~~creative~~ ✦ hardworking ✦ logical ✦ organized
> positive ✦ practical ✦ proactive

1. Someone who uses skills and imagination to make something new.   _creative_
2. Someone who is good at making or repairing things.   _____
3. Someone who can solve problems by thinking carefully.   _____
4. Someone who puts in effort and takes care of their work.   _____
5. Someone who controls a situation and does not just follow it.   _____
6. Someone who is happy and hopeful.   _____
7. Someone who plans their schedule well.   _____

Unit 3

Section 5 Speaking 1—Resume questionnaire

Exercise 1

▶ Fill in your own resume questionnaire below, circling the correct words. More than one answer can be chosen.

My resume questionnaire

1. Which of these adjectives would you use to describe yourself?
   creative   hardworking   logical   organized   positive   practical   proactive
   Other: _____
2. Which of these skills do you have?
   communication skills   computer skills   presentation skills   problem-solving skills
   organizational skills   teamwork   Other: _____
3. Which of these experiences do you have?
   internship   study abroad   part-time job   club activity   social circle   volunteer
   Other: _____
4. Do you have any licenses?
   driving license   teaching license   accounting license   bookkeeping license
   Other: _____
5. What are your interests?

6. What else can you say about yourself?

Exercise 2

▶ Interview a partner, circling the correct words in their resume questionnaire below.

My partner's resume questionnaire

1. Which of these adjectives would you use to describe yourself?
   creative   hardworking   logical   organized   positive   practical   proactive
   Other: _____
2. Which of these skills do you have?
   communication skills   computer skills   presentation skills   problem-solving skills
   organizational skills   teamwork   Other: _____
3. Which of these experiences do you have?
   internship   study abroad   part-time job   club activity   social circle   volunteer
   Other: _____
4. Do you have any licenses?
   driving license   teaching license   accounting license   bookkeeping license
   Other: _____
5. What are your interests?

6. What else can you say about yourself?

Exercise 3

▶ Together with your partner write six-sentence resumes for both of you, following the example below.

David's resume
Name: David Greene
Date of Birth: 20th December 2003
I am a logical and practical person. I have good problem-solving and organizational skills, and I am also quite good with computers. I studied abroad in Canada for six months in the second year at university, and I have had two part-time jobs. Unfortunately, I do not have any licenses yet, but I am planning to take my driving test soon. My interests include photography, and making and watching animation. I think I am a positive person because I always look forward to a new challenge.

My resume	My partner's resume
Name:	Name:
Date of Birth:	Date of Birth:
1.	1.
2.	2.
3.	3.
4.	4.
5.	5.
6.	6.

Part B

Section 1 Quiz

▶ Unscramble the sentences. There may be more than one answer.

1. am / at / communicating / good / I / not

_____.

2. being / community / good / in / involved / is / the

_____.

3. effort / important / in / is / it / put / to / with / work / your

_____.

4. customers / dealing / do / experience / have / I / much / not / with

_____.

5. at / be / good / explaining / should / teachers / things

_____.

6. good / have / I / my / presentation / said / skills / teacher

_____.

7. about / can / else / me / tell / what / you / yourself

_____?

8. after / education / graduate / I / I / in / to / want / work

_____.

9. are / at / good / making / people / practical / things

_____.

10. at / center / community / her / local / she / volunteers

_____.

Score: _____ / 10

| **Section 2** | Pronunciation—Stressed syllable in three-syllable words | 🎧 012 |

English words are separated by syllables:
英語の単語は音節で区切られています。

The word *banana* has three syllables.

The syllables are not equally stressed:
各音節に等しく強勢が置かれるわけではありません。

It's ba -Na -na, not BA − NA − NA.

Exercise 1   🎧 013

▶ The adjectives from **Section 4** of **Part A** have three syllables as follows:

cre-a-tive   hard-work-ing   log-i-cal   or-gan-ized
pos-i-tive   prac-ti-cal   pro-ac-tive

▶ Which syllable is stressed? Put the adjective in the correct column.

1st syllable	2nd syllable	3rd syllable

💬 Compare with a partner. Then practice saying the words.

Exercise 2   🎧 014

▶ Put the following adjectives into the correct column:

neg-a-tive   ro-man-tic   pop-u-lar   gen-er-ous   flex-i-ble
se-ri-ous   suc-cess-ful   tal-ent-ed   a-mus-ing   for-get-ful

1st syllable	2nd syllable	3rd syllable

💬 Which syllable is most commonly stressed? Which syllable is never stressed? Practice saying them with your partner.

Section 3 Listening

🎧 015, 016

Exercise 1

▶ Listen to two people talk to a careers officer about future jobs after graduating. What kind of job does the careers officer suggest?

Matthew	Jane
Suggested job:	Suggested job:
Reasons he is suitable: 1. 2. 3.	Reasons she is suitable: 1. 2. 3.

Exercise 2

▶ Why do you think each person is suitable for the job?

Section 4　Communication Strategy
— Asking for a more detailed explanation or clarification

Exercise 1　🎧 015, 016

▶ Listen to the conversations in **Section 3** of **Part B** again. How does the careers officer check his understanding? Choose the question type he asks from below:

> a. Can you explain (that) …?
> b. You mean …?
> c. What does "…" mean?
> d. Can you give me an example?

Exercise 2

▶ Complete the following conversations with the expressions from above:

Conversation 1

A: It says here that you have some sales experience. _____?

B: I have worked in a supermarket and in a clothing store.

A: _____ you've had two part-time jobs?

B: Three, actually. I also worked as a cleaner.

A: That's good. We need someone with work experience.

Conversation 2

A: Your resume says you are good with computers. _____ "good" _____?

B: Well, I can use different kinds of software.

A: _____?

B: Yes, I can use Excel and Word.

A: Excellent.

Exercise 3

▶ Have free conversations on these topics.

| Your perfect day | Your dream house | Your future plans | Your ideal trip |

Student A	Student B
• Choose one topic from above. • Try to talk about the topic for one or two minutes. • Leave a small break after each sentence.	• Listen carefully to your partner. • Ask your partner to explain in more detail when you think it is needed.

 Reverse roles and have two more conversations.

Section 5 Speaking 2

▶ Conversation Goal—Interview your partner for a job.
求職のための面接をしなさい。

Conversation Starter: What is your ideal job for the future?

Hints

- **Use the resume you have made for Speaking 1 of Part A (p. 30).**
- **Ask for clarification if you don't understand:** Can you explain …? You mean …? What does "…" mean?
- **Be careful with syllable stress:** LOgical, creAtive

Take notes about your partner(s) and present your results/findings to a group and/or the class.

Review 1

Exercise 1 Interview Test

▶ You will have a conversation with your teacher based on ONE of the following unit titles:
(Note: The unit title will be used as the conversation starter.)

    Unit 1: Are you still in touch with your friends from junior high?
    Unit 2: What do you do to stay healthy?
    Unit 3: What is your ideal job for the future?

☺ Look at the corresponding **Part B**; **Section 5**: **Speaking 2** for hints.

Exercise 2 Vocabulary

▶ Complete the puzzle. The black squares indicate a space.

Across
2. to decrease or lower the amount of something (verb)
4. in good physical condition (phrase)
5. having something in good order (adjective)
10. to stop communication with a friend (verb)
11. work in a company with no money to get experience (noun)
12. to meet somebody by chance (verb)

Down
1. working very hard (adjective)
3. very bad or serious; horrible (adjective)
6. using imagination and new ideas to make something (adjective)
7. having good health (adjective)
8. a group of people living in the same place (noun)
9. a vowel that is not stressed (noun)

Review **1**

Exercise 3 **Response**

▶ Write a suitable response or question that fits the conversation.

1. A: I have some bad news.

   B: _____ (rejoinder)

   A: I can't come to the party.

2. A: It looks cool outside today.

   B: _____ (rejoinder)

   A: Let's bring our jackets.

3. A: My brother won the game.

   B: _____ (rejoinder)

   A: Yeah. He was happy.

4. A: There's a new restaurant downtown.

   B: _____?

   A: It's an expensive sushi restaurant.

5. A: The weather at the beach was amazing last weekend.

   B: _____?

   A: With my two friends, John and Masa.

6. A: Saori got a new part-time job.

   B: _____?

   A: It's at a grocery store in the mall.

7. A: Japan has some very big cities.

   B: _____?

   A: Sure. Some examples are Tokyo, Osaka, and Nagoya.

8. A: My friend is thinking of going back to school.

   B: _____?

   A: I mean she wants to join a college or training program.

9. A: We have to use AI for our English class.

   B: _____?

   A: Yes, I can explain. It's a computer program that can talk with people.

Review 1

Exercise 4 Comprehension

🎧 017

▶ Tomohisa has prepared a short video recording for a health and fitness internship application at a gym in Australia.

Hello. My name is Tomohisa Yara. I am from Okinawa, but I have been studying sports science at university in Osaka for two years. I am interested in applying to join your health and fitness internship program.

Let me tell you a little about myself:
I like to stay in shape. I go to the gym three times a week, and I have been rowing since high school. Currently, I belong to the rowing club at university. We practice on Tuesdays, Thursdays, and the weekend. I am the club captain, so I have to be proactive and organized.

I hear Okinawan people are the healthiest in the world. One of the reasons is their healthy diet. Recently I have been experimenting with a new diet. I have cut out junk food, and I am more careful about the food I eat. Now I feel healthier than before.

I have been working part time at a coffee shop for more than a year. At work I have to deal with customers. I enjoy doing this, and my boss says I am good with people and have great communication skills.

My ideal job for the future is working as a trainer in a gym, or helping old people stay fit and healthy. By taking part in your internship program, I hope this can help my dream come true.

1. What kind of internship is Tomohisa applying for?

   _____

2. What does he do to stay in shape?

   _____

3. When does he practice rowing?

   _____

4. As club captain, what words does he use to describe himself?

   _____

5. Why are Okinawan people healthy?

   _____

Review 1

6. How has Tomohisa been experimenting with a new diet?

7. Has he only just started his part-time job at a coffee shop?

8. What does he enjoy doing at his part-time job?

9. What does Tomohisa's boss say about him?

10. What is his ideal job for the future?

Unit 4 What was the greatest day of your life?

Part A

Section 1 Opening Questions

▶ Ask your partner the following questions.

1. What is your earliest memory from when you were a child?
2. What is your best memory from high school? What happened?
3. What was the greatest day of your life?

Section 2 Useful Expressions

▶ Connect the expressions in **bold** to match them to the Japanese meaning.

1. Parents usually **attend** [列席する]
2. You do not have to **wear** [制服を着る]
3. In the UK, you **become** [大人になる]
4. It is common for parents to **compete** [～で競う]
5. Hina-matsuri is **the time** [～するとき]

a. **a uniform** in American high school.
b. **in** an event at Sports Day.
c. **a ceremony** when their children graduate from school.
d. **when** people wish for girls' happiness.
e. **an adult** at eighteen.

1. _____ 2. _____ 3. _____ 4. _____ 5. _____

40

Unit 4

Section 3 Model Conversation

Exercise 1

🎧 018

▶ Claire and Yoshiki are talking about memories. Listen to and read their conversation.

Claire: What's one of your happiest memories?

Yoshiki: I think that was (1)Seijin-no-hi.

Claire: (1)Seijin-no-hi? What's that?

Yoshiki: It's the day when (2)people celebrate becoming an adult.

Claire: So, what do people do?

Yoshiki: Well, they (3)go back to their hometown.

Claire: (4)Uh-huh.

Yoshiki: And they (5)attend a ceremony (6)with their elementary school friends.

Claire: (6)With their elementary school friends? And then what happens?

Yoshiki: (7)We take pictures and chat about old school days.

Claire: Sounds fun.

Exercise 2

▶ Practice the conversation with your partner. First, substitute the underlined parts in the model conversation as below. Next, try to substitute them with your own ideas.

Substitution	Your idea
1. Undo-kai	1. _____
2. children take part in sports day at school	2. _____
3. separate into two teams	3. _____
4. Okay	4. _____
5. compete	5. _____
6. in many different sporting events	6. _____
7. The team with the most points wins	7. _____

41

Section 4 **Language Focus**

Exercise 1

▶ Fill in the missing word using when, where, which, who, or why.

1. Christmas is the time __when__ people exchange cards and presents.

2. Can you remember the time _____ there were no smartphones?

3. I want to live in a place _____ there is a lot of nature.

4. Seijin-no-hi is the day _____ people celebrate becoming an adult.

5. Is this the train _____ goes to London?

6. The teacher does not like people _____ are always talking in class.

7. Can you tell me the reason _____ you are late?

8. A cemetery is a place _____ people bury their dead.

Exercise 2

▶ Add the correct preposition to complete the sentences.

1. I took part (_in_) a speech contest at high school.

2. I don't want to go back ( ) school.

3. It is common ( ) university students to work part time.

4. Masayuki went on a trip ( ) his girlfriend.

5. They went on a trip ( ) Kyoto.

6. He had a good time ( ) the party.

7. They are having a good time ( ) their classmates.

Unit 4

Section 5 Speaking 1—Missing information

[Student A] See page 71 for **Student B**

Exercise 1
🎧 019

▶ Read Passage 1 "The Day of the Dead."
Be prepared to answer your partner's questions.

Passage 1: The Day of the Dead

> The Day of the Dead is celebrated on November 1st and 2nd in Mexico and other Latin American countries. It is a special day to remember family members who have died. Many families visit cemeteries to put flowers on the graves and have picnics. There are also parades, where people wear costumes and paint their faces like skulls. The Day of the Dead looks scary, but it is a happy holiday because it celebrates the circle of life. That is why people use bright colors for decorations. There are also delicious sweets, shaped like skulls.

Exercise 2
🎧 020

▶ Read Passage 2 "St. Patrick's Day."
Think of four questions to ask your partner to find the missing information.

Passage 2: St. Patrick's Day

> St. Patrick's Day is celebrated on March 17th (where?)_____(1). It is a special day to celebrate the life of St. Patrick. He was the person who brought Christianity to Ireland. Many people celebrate St. Patrick's Day by (how?) _____(2). Green is the symbol of the day. People not only wear green, but they dye their food and drinks green. They eat green foods such as (what kind?) _____(3), and drink green beer. There are also a lot of (what?) _____(4) on this day to celebrate Irish culture.

(1) _____?
(2) _____?
(3) _____?
(4) _____?

Exercise 3

▶ Which festival would you prefer to experience? Discuss with your partner.

Part B

Section 1 Quiz

▶ Choose the correct words to complete the sentences.

> attend ✦ celebrate ✦ common ✦ earliest ✦ event
> separate ✦ symbol ✦ take part ✦ when ✦ where

1. It is not _____ for students to wear school uniforms in the U.S.A.

2. On April 1st many new students _____ an entrance ceremony.

3. My _____ memory is playing in the park with my father.

4. The cross is a _____ of Christianity.

5. On Sports Day we _____ into two teams: red and white.

6. The Edo period was a time _____ there were samurai.

7. Seki City is a place _____ knives are made.

8. At high school, I would often _____ in tennis matches.

9. Many different sporting _____s are held at the Olympics.

10. Young people _____ becoming adults at the age of twenty.

Score: _____ / 10

Section 2 Pronunciation—Intonation and rhythm in spoken English

Exercise 1
🎧 021

Look at the following sentence from the Model Conversation in **Section 3** of **Part A** (p. 41).

▶ Underline the words that are important to understand the meaning of the sentence.
文の意味を理解するために重要な単語（内容語）に下線を引きなさい。

It's the day when people celebrate becoming an adult.

▶ Underline with a wavy line the words that are important for the structure of the sentence.
文の構造に重要な単語（機能語）に波線を引きなさい。

It's the day when people celebrate becoming an adult.

▶ Listen to the sentence. The content words are stressed. The function words are not stressed.
文を聞きなさい。内容語は強勢され、機能語は強勢されません。

▶ Mark the stressed vowel in each of the content words. Check your answers with your partner.   e.g. cóntent

It's the day when people celebrate becoming an adult.

English is spoken with rhythm. The beat is the stress of the content word. Listen to the sentence again. Can you clap your hands to the rhythm of the sentence?
英文にはリズムがあり、内容語の強勢が拍子となります。英文のリズムに合わせて手拍子ができますか。

Exercise 2

▶ With a partner, repeat the process for the following three sentences. Identify the content words and identify the stressed syllable in each of those words. Listen to the audio and check your answers.

下の 3 つの文について、次のことを 2 人で確かめなさい。
①内容語はどれでしょう。②どの音節が強く発音されますか。③音声を聞いて答えをチェックしましょう。

   a. I took the train to France when I was young.
   b. I'd never been to such a wonderful place.
   c. Everything was different from my home country.

★Can you read them in rhythm one after the other without stopping?
途中で休まないで、リズムに乗って読めますか。

Exercise 3

▶ Take turns saying the sentences with your partner. One of you should clap the beat of the sentence. The other should try and match the sentence stress to the beat.

Section 3 Listening

Exercise 1

▶ Two people are looking at old photos. Listen to their conversation.

Exercise 2

▶ Listen to the conversation again. Read the statements and check whether they are true (T), false (F), or not sure (NS).

   1. Yumi went on a trip with two friends from high school.   _____
   2. Japanese high school students wear their uniforms on school trips.   _____
   3. Yumi did not like her own school uniform.   _____
   4. Yumi wanted to make good high school memories on her trip to DisneySea.   _____
   5. Yumi shows David three photographs.   _____
   6. In the second photograph they are riding a rollercoaster.   _____
   7. Yumi had a good time at DisneySea.   _____

| Section 4 | Communication Strategy—Shadowing: repeating key words to ask for detail |

Exercise 1

▶ Look at the Model Conversation from **Section 3** of **Part A** (p. 41). What key words were repeated + what question was asked for detail?

- _____

- _____

Exercise 2

▶ Look at the five example conversations. Fill in the missing parts with suitable statements, key words, follow-up questions, or answers.

1. A: I would like to visit some amusement parks.

   B: _____? Which ones?

   A: Well, I definitely want to go to USJ.

2. A: It takes me a long time to get to university.

   B: A long time? _____?

   A: Over one and a half hours.

3. A: I don't have much time on weekends.

   B: You don't have much time? What are you doing?

   A: _____.

4. A: _____.

   B: The USA? Where exactly?

   A: Well, I was born in New York, but I grew up in California.

5. A: I have been to many countries.

   B: _____? For example?

   A: I've traveled across Europe, and to America and Australia.

Exercise 3

▶ Have free conversations on these topics:

A teacher you like	A place you visited
An interesting experience you had	A valuable item you have

▶ Useful follow-up questions:

What do you mean?	Can you give me an example?	Please tell me more.
Can you explain that?	Where / When / What ... exactly?	

46

Unit 4

Student A	Student B
• Choose one topic from above. • Try to talk about the topic for one or two minutes. • Leave a small break after each sentence.	• Listen carefully to your partner. • Shadow (repeat key words) your partner and ask for more detail when you think it is needed.

 Reverse roles and have two more conversations.

Section 5 Speaking 2

▶ Conversation Goal—Have a conversation with your partner about the greatest day of your life. Decide whose day sounds more fun and think of two reasons why.
これまでの人生で最良の日はいつだったかについて会話しなさい。どちらのほうが楽しそうな日であったか、その理由を 2 つ考えましょう。

Conversation Starter: What was the greatest day of your life?

Hints

- **Use rejoinders to show you are listening:** Uh-huh. Right. Mm-hmm.
- **Shadow, and ask for detail:** Undo-kai? At kindergarten, or elementary school?
- **Try to speak with English rhythm. Stress content words, but not function words:** It's the **day** when **people celebrate becoming** an **adult**.

Take notes about your partner(s) and present your results/findings to a group and/or the class.

47

Unit 5 Where is somewhere you would like to visit?

Part A

Section 1 Opening Questions

▶ Ask your partner the following questions.

1. Where is somewhere you would like to visit?
2. What is something you have always wanted to do?
3. Which would you prefer, going to the mountains or going to the beach?
4. How do you like to spend a rainy day at home?

Section 2 Useful Expressions

▶ Connect the expressions in **bold** to match them to the Japanese meaning.

1. **Is it** [〜できますか？]
2. **Would you** [〜してもよろしいですか？]
3. **What** [〜してはどうでしょうか？]
4. **Could you** [〜かどうか教えてくださいませんか？]
5. **Would it** [〜しても構いませんでしょうか？]

a. **be okay if** we stay one more night?
b. **tell me if** this seat is taken?
c. **mind if** I open the window?
d. **if** we go by car?
e. **possible to** get there by train?

1. _____   2. _____   3. _____   4. _____   5. _____

48

Unit 5

Section 3 — Model Conversation

Exercise 1

🎧 024

▶ A woman and her visiting nephew are talking about weekend plans. Listen to and read their conversation.

Aunt: Where would you like to go this weekend?

Nephew: Would you mind going somewhere (1)different?

Aunt: Somewhere (1)different? What do you mean?

Nephew: We often go someplace (2)near here. Do you think we could (3)drive someplace far this time?

Aunt: What if we go to (4)the big city? There's a lot to (5)experience there.

Nephew: That sounds great! I have always wanted to (6)climb the TV tower.

Aunt: Would you like to stay all day?

Nephew: Definitely. Would it be okay if we (7)have dinner at a steak restaurant?

Aunt: Sure. Then we can really enjoy our time there.

Nephew: I agree.

Exercise 2

▶ Practice the conversation with your partner. First, substitute the underlined parts in the model conversation as below. Next, try to substitute them with your own ideas.

Substitution	Your idea
1. local	**1.** _____
2. far	**2.** _____
3. hang out around here	**3.** _____
4. Green State Park	**4.** _____
5. enjoy	**5.** _____
6. see the waterfall there	**6.** _____
7. go on a hiking trail	**7.** _____

49

Section 4 Language Focus

Exercise 1

▶ Choose a suitable verb and an adjective for the following situations: (more than one answer may be possible; be careful with singular/plural pronouns)

Verb	Adjective
look sound taste	good great nice bad strange amazing
smell feel seem	difficult fantastic terrible wonderful

1. **A:** Can you try this soup? I think it's a little salty.

   B: You're right. It _____ _____.

2. **A:** Have you seen these new designs? Aren't they great?

   B: Yes, they _____ _____.

3. **A:** Dinner is ready. Let's eat.

   B: Great. It _____ _____.

4. **A:** Have you heard that new K-pop group?

   B: Yeah, they _____ _____.

5. **A:** Are you Okay? You don't look well.

   B: No, I _____ _____.

6. **A:** Can you help me with my homework? I don't understand it.

   B: Probably not. It _____ _____.

7. **A:** What do you think of the new teacher? I think she's great.

   B: I agree. She _____ _____.

Exercise 2

▶ Rewrite the following questions (using the question starters in parentheses) to make them more polite.

1. Can I open the window? (Could I ...?)

   _____

2. Can I open the window? (Is it possible to ...?)

   _____

3. Can I open the window? (Would it be okay if …?)

___

4. Can I open the window? (Would you mind if …?)

___

5. Is there a post office near here? (Could you tell me if …?)

___

6. Do they sell stamps? (Do you know …?)

___

7. Where is the supermarket? (Do you know …?)

___

8. Where can I buy groceries? (Could you tell me …?)

___

Section 5 Speaking 1—Board game

▶ Play the board game with your partner. You will both need a marker and a coin.
Toss a coin to move forward: Head = 3 spaces; Tail = 2 spaces

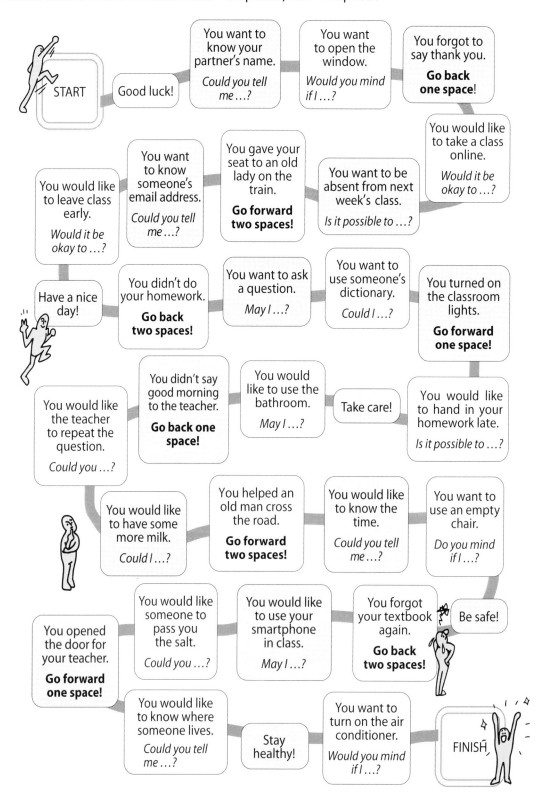

Part B

Section 1 — Quiz

▶ Circle the correct words to complete the sentences.

1. I would like to visit (somewhere / something) warm.
2. I really want to try (somewhere / something) spicy.
3. (Would / Should) you mind if I open the window?
4. (Would / Should) I take off my shoes?
5. A: Would you like to come shopping with me tomorrow?
   B: (Looks / Sounds) great!
6. A: What do you think of this new design?
   B: It (looks / sounds) wonderful.
7. Do you mind (to start / starting) early?
8. Is it possible (to start / starting) early?
9. Do you know (if / where) the supermarket is?
10. Do you know (if / where) the supermarket is open?

Score: _____ / 10

53

Section 2 — Pronunciation
—Assimilation of *you* with the auxiliary verbs *would*, *could*, *should*, and *did*

🎧 025

In spoken English, the word *you* is often assimilated with the auxiliary verbs *would*, *could*, *should*, and *did*. The *d* sound at the end of the auxiliary combines with *you* to make a *ju* sound. Note, this is true even when speaking politely.

助動詞 would、could、should、did の後に you がくる場合、助動詞の最後の d の音が you と同化して ju の音に変化します。丁寧に話す場合でも、同様に変化します。

e.g.
1. Did you finish your homework? → Diju finish your homework?
2. Would you mind opening the door? → Wouju mind opening the door?
3. Could you do me a favor? → Couju do me a favor?
4. Should you find a wallet, please tell the staff. → Shouju find a wallet, please tell the staff.

Exercise 1
🎧 026

▶ Listen to the following questions or statements. Some have assimilations, some do not. Check (✓) those where you can hear the assimilated *ju* sound.

1. Would you mind if I come home late?　(　)
2. Could you please tell me the time?　(　)
3. Where would you like to go?　(　)
4. You shouldn't do that, should you?　(　)
5. Did you have a nice vacation?　(　)
6. Which would you prefer, coffee or tea?　(　)
7. Could you open the door for me?　(　)
8. When did you arrive?　(　)

Exercise 2

▶ Practice reading the questions and statements with your partner. Try assimilating *you* each time.

Exercise 3

▶ Practice reading the Model Conversation from **Section 3** of **Part A** (p. 49). This time use the assimilated form of *you* where necessary.

Unit 5

Section 3 Listening

 027

▶ Taisei is on a homestay in Australia. Listen to him ask his host mother questions while sitting down to eat with her.

Exercise 1

▶ Listen to the conversation. Check (   ) the following polite questions Taisei uses.

1. Could I …?   (   )
2. Is it possible …?   (   )
3. Could you …?   (   )
4. Could you tell me …?   (   )
5. Do you know …?   (   )
6. Would you mind if …?   (   )
7. Would it be okay if …?   (   )

Exercise 2

▶ Listen to the conversation again. Read the statements and check whether they are true (T), false (F), or not sure (NS).

1. Today is Friday.   (   )
2. Meat pies are traditional Australian food.   (   )
3. Meat pies are made with gravy.   (   )
4. Taisei wants to make a meat pie.   (   )
5. The host mother would like Taisei to pass the pepper and salt. (   )
6. The host mother and Taisei are going to the supermarket together. (   )
7. The host mother is worried about leaving the door unlocked.   (   )
8. Taisei wants to eat breakfast later on Sunday.   (   )

Section 4 Communication Strategy—Making suggestions and adding support

Exercise 1

▶ Look at the Model Conversation from **Section 3** of **Part A** (p. 49). Can you identify where a suggestion is offered, followed by a support?

1. Suggestion: _____

   Support: _____

2. Suggestion: _____

   Support: _____

55

Exercise 2

▶ Look at the four example conversations. Complete the suggestion or add a support to complete the conversations.

1. **A:** I'm hungry.

   B: Why don't we _____? I heard the food there is really good.

   A: Good idea. I've never been there.

2. **A:** What shall we do tomorrow?

   B: How about _____? There is a sale on at the mall.

   A: Actually, I need some new shoes.

3. **A:** I don't feel very well today.

   B: Why don't you stay home? _____.

   A: Yes, you're probably right.

4. **A:** Did you hear Jane had a baby?

   B: Yes. Perhaps we could buy her something. _____?

   A: Yes, that would be nice.

Exercise 3

▶ Take turns making suggestions and adding support for the following situations:

You don't have enough money.	You don't have any free time.
You don't understand the homework.	You want to quit your school club.
You had an argument with your best friend.	You don't know what to do in the future.
You are going to be late for class.	You don't like the summer.

Student A	Student B
• Choose one situation from above. • Try to talk about the topic for one or two minutes. • React to your partner's suggestion.	• Make a suggestion and add a support.

💬 Reverse roles and have two more conversations.

Section 5 Speaking 2

▶ Conversation Goal—Make a plan with your partner to go on a trip together. Decide on the location, accommodation type, and three activities to do together.
2人で出かける旅行プランを考えなさい。出かける場所と宿泊先に加えて、一緒に行う3つの活動を決めましょう。

Conversation Starter: Where is somewhere you would like to visit?

 Hints

- **Make suggestions:** How about …? Why don't we …? Perhaps we could ….
- **React to positive ideas:** That sounds fun/amazing/wonderful/interesting.
- **Try to use some polite questions:** Do you know …? Would you mind …? Would it be okay …?

Take notes about your partner(s) and present your results/findings to a group and/or the class.

Unit 6 What is something you feel strongly about?

Part A

Section 1 Opening Questions

▶ Ask your partner the following questions. Remember to answer yes/no questions with extra information.

1. Do you think older people listen to young people's opinions?
2. What is something you feel strongly about?
3. What is something you disagree with?
4. What do you think about smoking?

Section 2 Useful Expressions

▶ Connect the expressions in **bold** to match them to the Japanese meaning.

1. Let me **make** [考えを述べる]
2. **How do you feel** [～をどう思う？]
3. I would like to **respond** [～に応える]
4. Do you know **what** [私が言いたいこと]
5. I strongly **disagree** [～に反対する]

a. **with** you.
b. **I mean**?
c. **to** your points.
d. **about** today's lesson?
e. **some points**, will you?

1. _____ 2. _____ 3. _____ 4. _____ 5. _____

58

Unit 6

Section 3 Model Conversation

Exercise 1
🎧028

▶ Taichi and Aoi are discussing university life. Listen to and read their conversation.

Taichi: How do you feel about (1)online classes?

Aoi: (2)I like them.

Taichi: Why do you say that?

Aoi: Well, (3)if there are too many students in class, it is difficult to hear.

Taichi: Yeah.

Aoi: Also, (4)I can listen to the online lecture again if I don't understand.

Taichi: Right.

Aoi: And most importantly, (5)I don't have to get up early in the morning! Don't you agree?

Taichi: No, I disagree. (6)I want to speak to the professor face to face.

Aoi: I know what you mean, but I can't change my opinion.

Taichi: I'm sorry. (7)I have to disagree with you.

Exercise 2

▶ Practice the conversation with your partner. First, substitute the underlined parts in the model conversation as below. Next, try to substitute them with your own ideas.

Substitution	Your idea
1. school uniforms	1. _____
2. I don't like them	2. _____
3. the rules are too strict	3. _____
4. the uniform is too cold in the winter	4. _____
5. I want to wear what I want	5. _____
6. I like wearing the same clothes as my friends	6. _____
7. I can't agree	7. _____

59

Section 4 Language Focus

Exercise 1

▶ Look at the explanatory follow-up sentence. Then choose words from each box to complete the sentence.

> ~~do~~ ✦ sit ✦ spend time
> study ✦ wake up ✦ wear

> how ✦ ~~what~~ ✦ what
> what ✦ when ✦ where

1. When I visit my grandfather, he always lets me (*do*)(*what*) I want. There aren't any rules!

2. At high school you cannot (   )(   ) you want. You must wear a uniform.

3. At university we can (   )(   ) we are interested in. I chose business and economics.

4. My English teacher lets us (   )(   ) we like. There isn't a seating plan.

5. On Fridays I can (   )(   ) I like because I don't have classes in the morning.

6. On Sundays, I can (   )(   ) I like. I don't need to go to school or my part-time job.

Exercise 2

▶ Respond to the following opinions stating whether the person agrees or disagrees based on their comments. Add adverbs for emphasis.

> completely ✦ totally ✦ personally ✦ strongly

1. **A:** Smoking should be banned in public places.

   B: I ___*totally*___ agree / ~~disagree~~. It is bad for other people's health.

2. **A:** Global warming is not a big problem.

   B: I _____ agree / disagree. It is the biggest problem in the world.

3. **A:** The USA is the greatest country in the world.

   B: I _____ agree / disagree. There are many problems in the USA.

4. **A:** No one really likes green peas.

   B: I _____ agree / disagree. They are horrible.

5. **A:** English is a fun subject.

   B: I _____ agree / disagree. We can communicate with people all over the world.

6. **A:** Globalization is finished.

   B: I _____ agree / disagree. Every country should produce their own goods and services.

Section 5 Speaking 1—Exchange of opinions

▶ Take turns stating your position verbally and adding follow-up support to the following statements. Your partner should respond to you and then add their support.

> **e.g.** A: I totally agree that SNS is bad for society. People should enjoy time in nature.
> B: I disagree. SNS has many good things, too. / I agree with you. It's a waste of time.

Love is the most important thing in the world.	SNS is bad for society.	AI will change the world.	People should only work four days a week.
Globalization is finished.	Video games are addictive.	The USA is the greatest country in the world.	Free time is more important than money.
Most people use their smartphones too much.	Men and women are equal.	Guns are not dangerous.	Global warming is not a serious problem.
People should vote from the age of 16.	China will be the most powerful country one day.	Japan is a safe country.	All countries should try to reach SDGs.

Part B

Section 1   Quiz

▶ Unscramble the sentences. There may be more than one answer.

1. don't / I / know / mean / what / you

_____.

2. I / like / points / respond / to / to / would / your

_____.

3. about / feel / is / something / strongly / what / you

_____?

4. agree / completely / I / opinion / with / your

_____.

5. banned / be / I / in / should / smoking / think / places / public

_____.

6. about / do / feel / global / how / warming / you

_____?

7. could / class / in / liked / sit / students / the / they / where

_____.

8. at / can / choose / study / to / university / we / we / want / what

_____.

9. disagree / have / I / to / with / you

_____.

10. let / make / me / points / some / will / you

_____?

Score: _____ / 10

Section 2 Pronunciation—Function words at the end

🎧 029

No stress is put on the final word in a sentence when it is a function word.
文の最後の単語が機能語なら強勢は置かれません。

▶ Look at the opening exchange from the Model Conversation in **Section 3** of **Part A** (p. 59).

　　　A: How do you feel about online classes?
　　　B: I like them.

▶ Identify the content words and the function words in the question and answer. Remember usually only content words are stressed. Listen to check the answer.

質問と答えの文中にある内容語と機能語を見つけなさい。通常、強勢されるのは内容語です。聞いてチェックしなさい。

Note that in the response 'I like them', both 'I' and 'them' are pronouns. Only the verb 'like' is stressed. Learners of English are likely to put stress on the first and last words, but this is not correct, and sounds very unnatural to native speakers.

上記の *I like them.* の *I* と *them* は代名詞（機能語）です。内容語である動詞の *like* だけに強勢が置かれます。学習者は最初と最後の単語に強勢を置いて発音しがちですが、ネイティブ・スピーカーにはとても不自然に聞こえます。

Exercise 1

▶ Listen to the following exchanges. Mark the stress in the question/statement and response.

A	B
1. What do you think of our new teacher?	I like her.
2. Your dog is very friendly.	He likes you.
3. What happened to the last cookie?	I ate it.
4. Did I introduce you to my classmates?	Yes, we met them.
5. Have you tidied your room?	Yeah, I did it.
6. It's going to snow tomorrow.	I heard that.
7. Classes are canceled today.	I know that.

💬 Take turns reading and responding in the exchanges. Make sure to put the stress in the correct place.

Exercise 2

 031

▶ Listen to the following exchanges. Write the responses.

A	B
1. The woman in the accident is my neighbor.	( ) ( ) ( )?
2. Manchester City won their game.	( ) ( ) ( ).
3. Do we have to do the homework by tomorrow?	( ) ( ) ( ).
4. Did your friends catch the last train?	( ) ( ) ( ).
5. This is the first dress I have ever made.	( ) ( ) ( )?
6. Do you like living here?	( ) ( ) ( ).

▶ Take turns reading and responding in the exchanges. Make sure to put the stress in the correct place.

Section 3 Listening

 032

▶ Two groups of students are having a debate on social media in Professor Greene's discussion class. One group is responding to the previous group's points.

Exercise 1

▶ What type of response is it? (expert opinion / common knowledge / personal experience) Write them in the 2nd column.
2つ目の欄に、どのような種類の応答かを書き入れなさい。(expert opinion：専門家の意見、common knowledge：常識、personal experience：個人的な経験)

Point	Type of response (expert opinion / common knowledge / personal experience)	Response
1. Young people spend too much time on social media.		
2. Students use social media when they should be studying.		
3. Social media makes us unhealthy.		

Unit 6

Exercise 2

▶ What expressions does the speaker use to respond to the previous speaker's points?

> **e.g.** A recent study said that ….   Does he know that …?   Everyone knows ….

✎ Write them in the 3rd column.

Section 4 Communication Strategy—Getting people to respond

Exercise 1

▶ Look at the Model Conversation from **Section 3** of **Part A** (p. 59).

What expressions to get a response were used from below?

_____

> What do you think about (that)?
>
> How do you feel about (that)?
>
> Do you know what I mean?
>
> Don't you agree?
>
> Why do you say that?

Exercise 2

▶ Complete the following conversations with the expressions from above. There may be more than one answer.

Conversation 1

A: Tell me: (1)_____ our new teacher?

B: He seems very nice. Why?

A: Well, I think he is difficult to understand. (2)_____?

B: Yeah, I guess you're right. He does speak very quickly.

A: Do you think I can ask him to speak more slowly?

B: Why not? I don't think he will mind.

Conversation 2

A: This class has too much homework. (3)_____?

B: Not really. We need to read every day to improve our TOEIC score.

A: But I don't have time for my other classes. (4)_____?

B: Well, yes, I know what you mean. That is why I quit my part-time job.

A: Huh? I need more free time.

65

▶ State your opinions on these topics:

| Artificial Intelligence (AI) | 4-day working week |
| wearing masks | Japan's declining population |

Student A	Student B
• Choose one topic from above, state your opinion, and ask for a response.	• Listen carefully to your partner and respond to their opinion.

 A: How do you feel about American gun laws? I think there is too much gun crime in the US. People should not be able to buy guns. Do you agree?
B: Yes, I totally agree. We do not need guns.

Reverse roles and have two more conversations.

 Speaking 2

▶ Conversation Goal—Have a discussion about something you feel strongly about. Give three reasons to support your opinion.
あなたが強く思っていることについて話し合いなさい。自分の意見を支持する理由を3つあげましょう。

Conversation Starter: What is something you feel strongly about?

Hints

- You can use the topics from Speaking 1 of Part A (p. 61).
- Be careful with sentence stress.
- **Ask your partner to respond:** How do you feel about that? Don't you agree?
- **Use adverbs for emphasis:** I **completely** agree. I **totally** disagree.

Take notes about your partner(s) and present your results/findings to a group and/or the class.

Review 2

Exercise 1 Interview Test

▶ You will have a conversation with your teacher based on ONE of the following unit titles:
(*Note: The unit title will be used as the conversation starter.*)

　　Unit 4: What was the greatest day of your life?
　　Unit 5: Where is somewhere you would like to visit?
　　Unit 6: What is something you feel strongly about?

😊 Look at the corresponding **Part B**; **Section 5**: **Speaking 2** for hints.

Exercise 2 Vocabulary

▶ Complete the puzzle. The black squares indicate a space.

Across
3. something you remember from the past (noun)
5. continuing something for a long time (adjective)
8. showing good manners and respect (adjective)
9. to join an activity (phrase)
11. to meet people for a happy day/event (verb)
12. feeling something in a powerful way (adverb)

Down
1. something you do but cannot stop; e.g. drugs (adjective)
2. can be done (adjective)
4. to have a different opinion (verb)
6. to have the same opinion (verb)
7. a view or belief, but not a fact (noun)
10. wonderful or fantastic (adjective)

Review *2*

Exercise 3 Response

▶ Write a suitable response or question that fits the conversation.

1. A: Anna booked a vacation to Hawaii.

   B: _____? _____?

   A: She is going next June.

2. A: David joined a sports gym.

   B: _____? _____?

   A: It costs about 7,000 yen a month.

3. A: My mother gave me a dog for my birthday.

   B: _____? _____?

   A: It is a Shiba.

4. Let's play video games after class.

   _____ (add support)

5. Would you like to go to a movie?

   _____ (add support)

6. Why don't you get some rest?

   _____ (add support)

7. I don't think love is important.

   _____? (get response)

8. Young people use smartphones too much.

   _____? (get response)

9. I hated wearing a school uniform.

   _____? (get response)

Review 2

Exercise 4 Comprehension

▶ Tomohisa has prepared a summary report after his internship in Australia.

Background
I did a four-week health and fitness internship in Brisbane on the Gold Coast, Australia. I stayed with a host family: Mr. and Mrs. Fletcher and their 15-year-old son, Damien.

Good points
- Working at the gym has been the greatest experience in my life. The staff were so friendly and helpful. They taught me a lot, and we often went out together in the evenings. My best memory is going to karaoke with them.
- The Gold Coast is a place where there is beautiful nature. I took lots of pictures of the beach and sea!
- Playing video games with Damien was great fun!

Bad points
- Communicating with people was sometimes difficult. It was not possible to understand everything they said. One reason is that Australian pronunciation is very different from the American pronunciation I learned. I often had to say, "Could you repeat that, please?"
- I did not agree with some of their house rules. Can you believe I could only take a shower for 10 minutes?

Advice for future students
There are two points I want to make:
- You should study English seriously before you do an international internship.
- On the weekend you can do what you like. There is a lot to experience in Brisbane, so go out and enjoy yourself!

1. What kind of internship did Tomohisa do?
   _____

2. Did Tomohisa enjoy working at the gym?
   _____

3. What is his best memory?
   _____

4. What is the Gold Coast like?
   _____

Review 2

5. What does Tomohisa say was great fun?
   _____

6. Why does Tomohisa think it is difficult to communicate with Australians?
   _____

7. What house rule did he disagree with?
   _____

8. What can future internship students do on the weekend?
   _____

9. What does Tomohisa advise students to do before an international internship?
   _____

10. Do you agree with this advice?
    _____

Unit 4 What was the greatest day of your life?

Part A

Section 5 Speaking 1—Missing information

[Student B] See page 43 for **Student A**

Exercise 1   🎧 019

▶ Read Passage 1 "The Day of the Dead."
  Think of four questions to ask your partner
  to find the missing information.

Passage 1: The Day of the Dead

The Day of the Dead is celebrated on (when?)_____(1) in Mexico and other Latin American countries. It is a special day to remember (what?)_____(2). Many families visit cemeteries to put flowers on the graves and have picnics. There are also parades, where people (what?)_____(3). The Day of the Dead looks scary, but it is a happy holiday because (why?)_____(4). That is why people use bright colors for decorations. There are also delicious sweets, shaped like skulls.

(1) _____?
(2) _____?
(3) _____?
(4) _____?

Exercise 2   🎧 020

▶ Read Passage 2 "St. Patrick's Day."
  Be prepared to answer your partner's questions.

Passage 2: St. Patrick's Day

St. Patrick's Day is celebrated on March 17th in Ireland and in the USA. It is a special day to celebrate the life of St. Patrick. He was the person who brought Christianity to Ireland. Many people celebrate St. Patrick's Day by wearing something green. Green is the symbol of the day. People not only wear green, but they dye their food and drinks green. They eat green food such as green hot dogs, green cookies, and green bread, and drink green beer. There are also a lot of festivals and parades on this day to celebrate Irish culture.

Exercise 3

▶ Which festival would you prefer to experience? Discuss with your partner.

Glossary

- Useful Expressions
- Words & Phrases

❧ Useful Expressions ❧

各ユニットの "**Section 2: Useful Expressions**" を英和（アルファベット順）と和英（アイウエオ順）に整理しました。文単位ではないので、辞書に掲載されている表記に準じて一部変更してあります。意味を忘れたとき、確認したいときに利用してください。

［英和索引］

attend a ceremony	列席する
be good at 〜	〜するのが得意
be good with 〜	〜の扱いがうまい
be involved in 〜	〜と関わり合う
become an adult	大人になる
bump into 〜	〜と偶然出会う
compete in 〜	〜で競う
Could you tell me if 〜?	〜かどうか教えてくださいませんか？
disagree with 〜	〜に反対する
drop 〜 a line	〜に連絡する
experiment with 〜	〜を試してみる
have been up to 〜	〜していた
have good communication skills	コミュニケーション力がある
How do you feel about 〜?	〜をどう思う？
in good health	健康で
Is it possible to 〜	〜できますか？
keep in touch with 〜	〜と連絡を取り合う
look good for one's age	年の割には元気そう
lose contact	連絡が取れなくなる
make some points	考えを述べる
out of shape	体調が悪い
put in effort with 〜	〜に努力を注ぐ
respond to 〜	〜に応える
skip a meal	食事を抜く
the time when 〜	〜するとき
wear a uniform	制服を着る
what I mean	私が言いたいこと
What if 〜?	〜してはどうでしょうか？
Would it be okay if 〜?	〜しても構いませんでしょうか？
Would you mind if 〜?	〜してもよろしいですか？

[和英索引]

大人になる	become an adult
〜かどうか教えてくださいませんか？	Could you tell me if 〜？
考えを述べる	make some points
健康で	in good health
コミュニケーション力がある	have good communication skills
〜していた	have been up to 〜
〜してはどうでしょうか？	What if 〜？
〜しても構いませんでしょうか？	Would it be okay if 〜？
〜してもよろしいですか？	Would you mind if 〜？
食事を抜く	skip a meal
〜するとき	the time when 〜
〜するのが得意	be good at 〜
制服を着る	wear a uniform
体調が悪い	out of shape
〜で競う	compete in 〜
〜できますか？	Is it possible to 〜
〜と関わり合う	be involved in 〜
〜と偶然出会う	bump into 〜
年の割には元気そう	look good for one's age
〜と連絡を取り合う	keep in touch with 〜
〜に応える	respond to 〜
〜に努力を注ぐ	put in effort with 〜
〜に反対する	disagree with 〜
〜に連絡する	drop 〜 a line
〜の扱いがうまい	be good with 〜
列席する	attend a ceremony
連絡が取れなくなる	lose contact
私が言いたいこと	what I mean
〜を試してみる	experiment with 〜
〜をどう思う？	How do you feel about 〜？

♣ Words & Phrases ♣

テキストにある英文の内容を理解するのに必要と思われる語彙をアルファベット順に一覧できるようにしました。
意味がわからないときに利用してください。

【A】

a couple of 〜	いくつかの〜、2 つの〜
accommodation	宿泊設備
accounting	会計学
actually	実際に、実は
addictive	中毒性の
adjective	形容詞
adverb	副詞
AI	人工知能（artificial intelligence）
air conditioner	エアコン
amazing	ものすごい、びっくりするような
amount	量
amusement park	遊園地
amusing	おもしろい
anyway	ともかく、いずれにしても
application	応募、申請
apply for 〜	〜に応募する
appropriate	適切な
architect	建築家
argument	口論
article	冠詞
as well	なおその上に、〜もまた
assignment	課題
assimilate	同化、融合する
assimilation	同化、融合
audio	音声
auxiliary verb	助動詞

【B】

ban	禁止する
barbecue	バーベキュー
based on 〜	〜に基づいて
bathroom	（個人宅の）トイレ
be on a diet	減量している
board game	ボードゲーム

book	予約する
bookkeeping	簿記
break	小休止
Brisbane	ブリスベン（オーストラリアの都市）
bury	埋める

【C】

cancel	取り消す、取りやめる
careers officer	職業相談員、就職係
catch up	追いつく、近況を伝え合う
celebrate	祝う
cemetery	共同墓地
Christianity	キリスト教
clap	（手を）たたく
clarification	明確化、説明
clothing store	衣料品店
comment	コメント、見解
common	普通の、ありふれた
commonly	一般に、普通には
complain	不平を言う
complete	完成する
completely	完全に
conjunction	接続詞
consider	熟慮する、検討する
contact	連絡する
contracted form	縮約形
content word	内容語
contraction	短縮、収縮
convert	変換する
convey	伝える
countable	数えられる、加算の
cross	十字架
customer	客
cut down on 〜	〜の量／数を減らす
cut out	（飲酒・喫煙などを）やめる

【D】

date of birth	生年月日
dead	死者
deal with ～	～に対応する
debate	ディベート
decline	低下する、衰える
decoration	装飾、飾りつけ
definitely	絶対に、確実に
definition	定義
describe	描写する、述べる
detailed	詳細な
do me a favor	お願いがある
driving license	運転免許証
dye	染める

【E】

emphasis	強調
empty	空いている
encourage	励ます
equal	平等の
equally	等しく
equipment	設備
especially	とりわけ
excellent	優れた、すばらしい
exchange	交換する；（会話の）やり取り
experience	経験；経験する
expert	専門家；専門的な
explanatory	説明的な
expression	表現

【F】

face to face	対面で
fantastic	すばらしい
fill in	記入する、書き入れる
finally	最後に
flexible	柔軟性のある、融通のきく
follow	従う
follow-up question	追加の質問
forgetful	忘れっぽい
forward	前に、先へ
function word	機能語

【G】

generous	寛大な、気前のよい
global warming	地球温暖化
globalization	国際化
grade	成績
gravy	肉汁、グレイビー
guess	推測する、言いあてる
gymnast	体操選手

【H】

hand in ～	～を提出する、手渡す
hang out	ぶらぶらして時を過ごす
hardworking	勤勉な
have a fever	熱がある
have ～ in common	共通点がある
head	（コインの）表
Hold on.	待て。
horrible	実にひどい、ぞっとする
How's it going?	調子はどう？元気？

【I】

identify	確認する、見つける
in touch with ～	～（人）と連絡して
include	含む
injure	傷つける
internship	研修、インターンシップ
intonation	イントネーション
Ireland	アイルランド
item	品目

【J】

junk food	ジャンクフード、ファーストフード

【K】

kindergarten	幼稚園

【L】

license	免許、免許証
location	場所
logical	論理的な
Long time, no see.	久し振りですね。
lose weight	体重が減る

【M】

mall	（歩行者専用の）商店街
media	メディア
missing	欠けている、不明の
mostly	たいていは
musical instrument	楽器

【N】

negative	消極的な
neighbor	隣人
No way!	とんでもない！まさか！
No worries.	心配ご無用。
note	注目する

【O】

oily	油っこい
Okinawan	沖縄の、沖縄人の
online	オンラインの、オンラインで
order	注文する
organizational	組織的な
organized	てきぱきとした、有能な

【P】

parentheses	括弧
personality	性格、個性
personally	個人的に
photo, photograph	写真
photography	写真撮影、写真術
phrase	慣用句、熟語
plural	複数の
polite	丁寧な
position	立場
positive	積極的な
practical	実用的な
predict	予測する
preposition	前置詞
present	述べる、発表する
present perfect	現在完了形
present tense	現在時制
previous	前の
proactive	率先的な
problem solving	問題解決

process	過程、手順
pronoun	代名詞
pronunciation	発音

【Q】

qualifier	修飾語句
questionnaire	アンケート、質問事項
quit	やめる

【R】

recent	最近の
recipe	レシピ、調理法
rejoinder	応答
repair	修理する
reply	返答する
reproduce	再生する
resume	身上書、履歴書
retail	小売り
reverse	逆にする
rewrite	書き直す
rhythm	リズム
rollercoaster	ローラーコースター
row	ボートをこぐ

【S】

salty	塩っ辛い
scary	恐ろしい、怖い
schedule	スケジュール
schwa	あいまい母音
SDGs	持続可能な開発目標（Sustainable Development Goals）
seating	座席の配列
separate	分ける、分かれる
serious	深刻な
seriously	本気に、真面目に
shadowing	（音の）後追い
Should you ～	万一～であれば（= If you should ～）
singular	単数の
situation	状況、場面
skill	技能、技術

skull	頭蓋骨
starter	始める言葉・話題
state	述べる
statement	発言、声明
stay in contact	連絡を取り続ける
stay in shape	体調を維持する
strategy	戦略、方略
stress	強勢；強勢を置く
study abroad	海外留学；海外に留学する
substitute	置き換える
substitution	置換、代入
suggest	提案する
suggestion	提案
suitable	適した、ふさわしい
syllable	音節

【T】

tail	（コインの）裏
take care	気をつける、注意する
take notes	メモする
take part in ～	～に参加する
take turns	交替する
talented	有能な
taste ～	～の味がする
teaching assistant	学生助手、教員補助学生
terrible	ひどい、ひどく悪い
the UK	大英帝国、イギリス
to be honest	正直なところ
toss	投げ上げる、ほうる
totally	まったく、すっかり
tough	つらい、骨の折れる
traditional	伝統的な
trail	（ハイキングなどの）コース、小道
trait	特性、特徴

【U】

unfortunately	あいにく、不運にも
unlocked	鍵のかかっていない
unscramble	正しく並べ替える

【V】

valuable	価値のある
vegetable	野菜
verb	動詞
verbally	言葉で
view	見解、考え
voice	有声音化する、声に出す
volunteer	志願する；ボランティア
vote	投票する
vowel	母音

【W】

waterfall	滝
wavy line	波線
Well done!	よかった！よくやった！

ベーシック・コミュニケーション　ブック2

2024 年 8 月 20 日　　第 1 刷発行

著　者	Julyan Nutt（ジュリアン・ナット）
	Adam Huston（アダム・ヒューストン）
	宮田 学（みやた　まなぶ）
	倉橋洋子（くらはし　ようこ）
発行者	前田俊秀
発行所	株式会社　三修社

〒 150-0001 東京都渋谷区神宮前 2-2-22
TEL 03-3405-4511　　FAX 03-3405-4522
振替 00190-9-72758
https://www.sanshusha.co.jp
編集担当 三井るり子・伊藤宏実

印刷・製本　日経印刷株式会社

©2024 Printed in Japan ISBN978-4-384-33536-1 C1082
表紙デザイン―やぶはなあきお
本文デザイン＆ DTP ― Shibasaki Rie
本文イラスト―高橋ユウ（p.12, 14, 22, 24, 28, 33, 34, 39, 51, 53, 61, 70）
準拠音声制作―高速録音株式会社
（吹込：Howard Colefield / Karen Haedrich / Chris Koprowski / Jennifer Okano）

JCOPY 〈出版者著作権管理機構 委託出版物〉
本書の無断複製は著作権法上での例外を除き禁じられています。複製される場合は、
そのつど事前に、出版者著作権管理機構（電話 03-5244-5088 FAX 03-5244-5089
e-mail: info@jcopy.or.jp）の許諾を得てください。